FARMYARD STORIES
The Goat

Kingfisher Books, Grisewood & Dempsey Ltd,
Elsley House, 24–30 Great Titchfield Street,
London W1P 7AD

This reformatted edition first published in 1992
by Kingfisher Books
2 4 6 8 10 9 7 5 3 1

Originally published in 1989 in paperback as
Farm Animal Stories: The Goat by Kingfisher Books

Copyright © Grisewood & Dempsey Ltd 1989, 1992

BRITISH LIBRARY CATALOGUING IN PUBLICATION DATA
A catalogue record for this book is available from the British Library

ISBN 0 86272 985 8

Series adviser: Dr Bryan Howard, University of Sheffield
Edited by Jacqui Bailey and Veronica Pennycook
Cover design by Cooper/Wilson
Cover illustration by Steve Holden/*John Martin & Artists Ltd*
Phototypeset by Southern Positives and Negatives
(SPAN), Lingfield, Surrey
Printed in Portugal

FARMYARD STORIES

The Goat

By Angela Royston
Illustrated by Eric Robson

Kingfisher Books

The white goat pushes her head through the fence and reaches for some tasty dandelions in the next field. It is autumn and the evening air is cool. Her udders feel heavy for they are full of milk.

Soon she ambles over to the other goats waiting at the gate. As the farmer opens the gate, the leader of the herd pushes through and all the other goats follow her to the milking shed.

The white goat waits in the little yard for her turn to be milked. She jostles a brown goat aside and goes through the narrow door. She climbs up the ramp and takes her place on the milking machine.

The farmer puts rubber cups over her teats.
The machine hums and clicks and she can feel
her udders emptying of milk as she munches
her food. Then she goes to the barn and settles
for the night.

The next morning the goats are let out into a
new field. They run across the grass and
explore it. The white goat and her sister jump
up in the air and then climb to the top of a
rocky mound. Her sister soon wanders off to
eat some dock leaves.

The white goat does not like dock and
stretches up into the hawthorn tree instead.
She eats the leaves and reaches for some red
berries. She puts her front feet onto a low
branch, then with a quick jump she climbs
right up into the tree.

The days get colder. The leaves fall and the grass dies back. The white goat and her sister are chewing their cud. After swallowing their food, they bring it back from their stomachs and chew it slowly.

Soon it begins to rain. The white goat's hair
quickly becomes wet and she starts to shiver
with cold. She gets to her feet and follows her
sister and the other goats as they move
towards the shelter of the barn.

One day the farmer puts the white goat into a pen with a large billy goat. The billy goat knows that she is ready to mate. He nuzzles her side and makes a chattering noise to her. The white goat sniffs his long beard. It has a very strong smell. The billy goat touches her face with his own and then they mate.

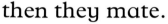

The winter days are cold and windy, and the goats stay in the barn nearly all the time. Sometimes the farm dog comes in to get warm. The goats are curious and try to sniff this strange animal.

All winter two baby kids are growing inside the white goat. Her body becomes large and heavy. She has less milk in her udders now, and about fourteen weeks after mating she is no longer milked at all.

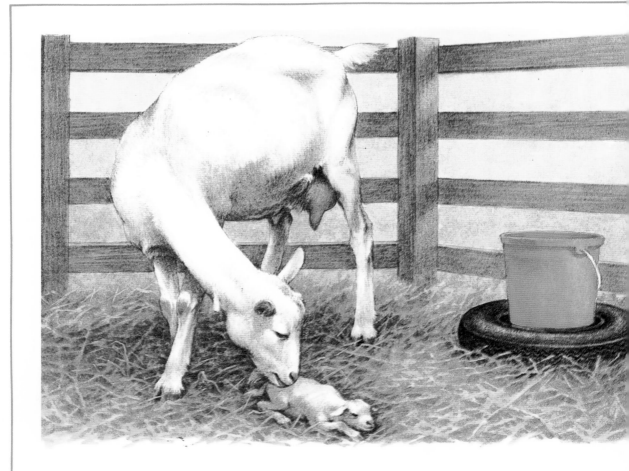

Five months after mating the kids are ready to
be born. The white goat is put into a stall of
her own with lots of fresh straw. A billy kid is
born first. She licks him all over and soon he
starts bleating. A few minutes later a nanny
kid is born.

Almost at once the new kids stand up on their wobbly legs. They lean against their mother and nuzzle her teats, searching for milk. Soon they are sucking eagerly. They quickly become stronger and in a few days they are skipping about.

When the kids are nearly a week old, the farmer takes the mother goat to be milked. The kids are put into a new stall with other young kids who feed from teats attached to a bucket of milk.

At first the kids feel strange and miss their
mother. They bleat and stay still, watching
the other kids prancing about. But by the next
day they feel more at home and begin to play
with the other kids.

The white goat misses her kids. She bleats loudly for them. But it is spring now and, after milking, the farmer takes her outside with the rest of the herd.

Her sister is with the herd and they playfully butt each other and jump about in the spring air. They are happy to have fresh grass and new leaves to eat.

More About Goats

The goat in this story is a Saanen. This breed first came from Switzerland and is very popular since it gives large quantities of milk.

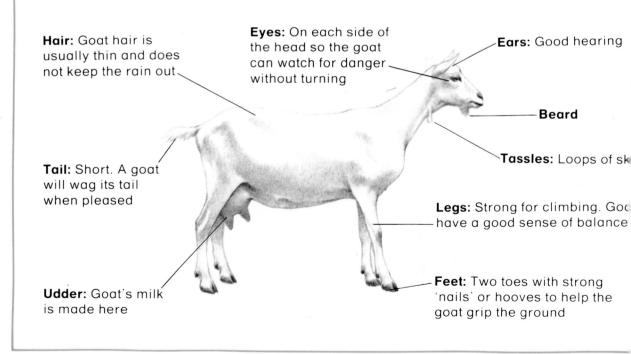

Hair: Goat hair is usually thin and does not keep the rain out

Eyes: On each side of the head so the goat can watch for danger without turning

Ears: Good hearing

Beard

Tassles: Loops of sk

Tail: Short. A goat will wag its tail when pleased

Legs: Strong for climbing. Goo have a good sense of balance

Udder: Goat's milk is made here

Feet: Two toes with strong 'nails' or hooves to help the goat grip the ground

Anglo Nubian

Toggenburg

British Alpine

Angora

Most goat farmers keep several different kinds of goat. Anglo Nubian goats give a milk with lots of fat in it which is good for making cheese. Alpine and Toggenburg goats were bred for mountainous countries. Angora goats have long fine hair which can be spun and knitted like sheep's wool.

Goats are browsers. They eat leaves, twigs, fruit and thistles as well as grass. They will climb almost anywhere to reach their favourite plants.

Some Special Words

Billy goat A male goat. Male goats are usually bigger then females. The horns are removed from females but billy goats often keep their horns.

Cud Goats do not chew their food as they browse. It is stored in two of their four stomachs. Later on they bring small cuds of it back into their mouths. They chew it until the cud is a mushy pulp, then they swallow it again.

Herd A group of goats. One goat leads the herd and the other goats follow her. The leader goes first to be milked. Sheepdogs cannot be used to round up goats since goats spread out when alarmed.

Kid A young goat. A mother usually gives birth to twins. Kids can stand and even walk a few minutes after being born.

Nanny goat A female goat.